Math Masters

Number and Operations in Base Ten

High-Speed Trains

Use Place Value Understanding and Properties of Operations to Add and Subtract

Julie Swenson

PowerKiDS press™

NEW YORK

Published in 2015 by The Rosen Publishing Group, Inc.
29 East 21st Street, New York, NY 10010

Book Design: Mickey Harmon

Photo Credits: Cover Shi Yali/Shutterstock.com; p. 5 SeanPavonePhoto/Shutterstock.com; p. 7 Tupungato/
Shutterstock.com; p. 9 http://en.wikipedia.org/wiki/File:JRW-500-nozomi.jpg; p. 11 http://en.wikipedia.org/wiki/File:JR-
Maglev-MLX01-2.jpg; p. 13 Regien Paassen/Shutterstock.com; p. 15 (map) Alfonso de Tomas/Shutterstock.com; p. 15
(train) m.bonotto/Shutterstock.com; p. 17 Rostislav Glinksy/Shutterstock.com; pp. 19, 21 Hung Chung Chih/
Shutterstock.com; p. 22 pedrosala/Shutterstock.com.

Swenson, Julie.
High-speed trains: use place value understanding and properties of operations to add and subtract / by Julie Swenson.
  p. cm. — (Math masters: number and operations in base ten)
Includes index.
ISBN 978-1-4777-4759-9 (pbk.)
ISBN 978-1-4777-4761-2 (6-pack)
ISBN 978-1-4777-6403-9 (library binding)
1. Place value (Mathematics) — Juvenile literature. 2. Addition — Juvenile literature. 3. Subtraction — Juvenile literature.
4. High speed trains — Juvenile literature. I. Title.
QA141.3 S94 2015
513.5—d23

Manufactured in the United States of America

CPSIA Compliance Information: Batch #WS15RC: For further information contact Rosen Publishing, New York, New York at 1-800-237-9932.

Contents

On the Move!

Trains have been a **popular** form of **transportation** for almost 200 years. However, as more people began traveling by car and airplane in the 20th century, railroad companies needed to find new ways to **attract** travelers. One way they did this was by building high-speed trains. These trains are popular in Europe and Asia, and they can get people from city to city very quickly!

Japan was one of the first countries to use high-speed trains, which are sometimes called bullet trains.

Japanese Bullet Trains

The first Japanese bullet trains began running in 1964, and they were a big success. The Hayabusa ("Falcon") train was introduced in 2011, and it can reach speeds of more than 185 miles (298 km) per hour.

Can you add 10 to 185 in your head? It's the same as adding 1 to the number in the tens place. That equals 195.

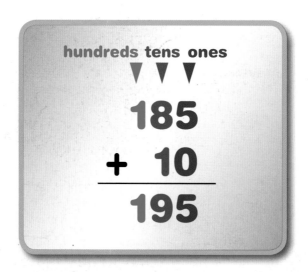

In the number 185, the number in the tens place is 8.
When you add 1 to 8, you get 9. That's why 185
plus 10 equals 195.

While some bullet trains can go more than 185 miles per hour, they commonly travel at a slower **average** speed. The 500 Series Nozomi train reached an average speed of about 163 miles (262 km) per hour. That's a record for the fastest average speed on a train trip!

Can you subtract 10 from 163 in your head? The answer is 153.

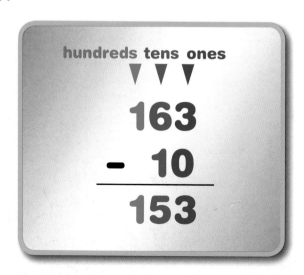

When you subtract 10 from a given number, you subtract 1 from the number in the tens place. In this case, you subtract 1 from 6.

9

Moving Without Wheels

Some Japanese trains don't even have wheels. They're called maglev trains. They use **magnets** to lift them above the tracks and push them along. In 2003, 1 of these trains reached a speed of 361 miles (581 km) per hour.

If you wanted to add 100 to 361, you would only need to add 1 to the number in the hundreds place, which is 3. That makes 461.

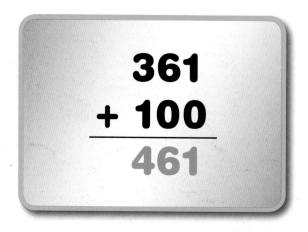

$$361 + 100 \over 461$$

Maglev trains are still being tested in Japan. They aren't used to carry people yet.

European Trains

Germany is also building maglev trains. German maglev trains aren't carrying people yet either. Instead, Germans travel on the Intercity Express (ICE) high-speed train system. Some of these trains can go as fast as 174 miles (280 km) per hour.

How can you subtract 100 from 174 in your head? You take 1 away from the number in the hundreds place.

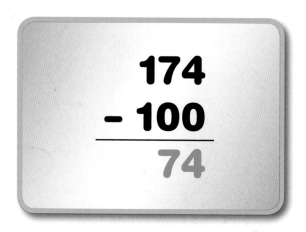

$$174 - 100 = 74$$

When you take 1 away from the hundreds place in the number 174, you're left with 0 hundreds. That's why 174 minus 100 equals 74.

High-speed trains are also popular in other European countries, such as Italy. In 1992, a track was built to carry people from Rome to Florence. The trains that run on this track travel at a top speed of 185 miles (298 km) per hour. If a train were to go 10 miles per hour less than 185, it would be going 175 miles per hour.

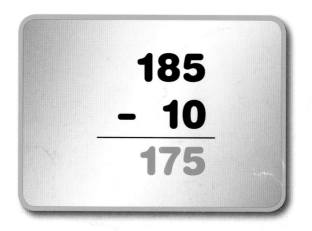

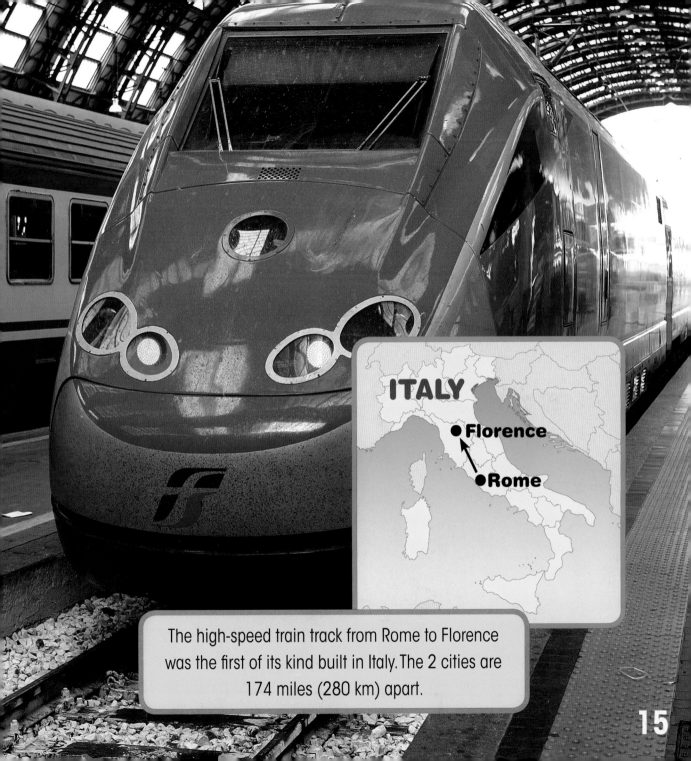

ITALY

● Florence

● Rome

The high-speed train track from Rome to Florence was the first of its kind built in Italy. The 2 cities are 174 miles (280 km) apart.

Someday an Italian high-speed train might travel even faster than 185 miles per hour. If a train traveled at 195 miles per hour, and you added 10 miles per hour to that speed in your head, you would get 205 miles per hour. In order to add these numbers, you have to regroup and carry in your head. It's easy!

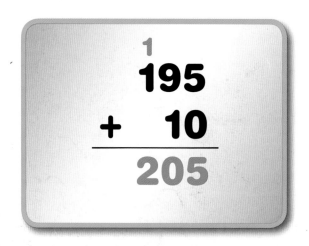

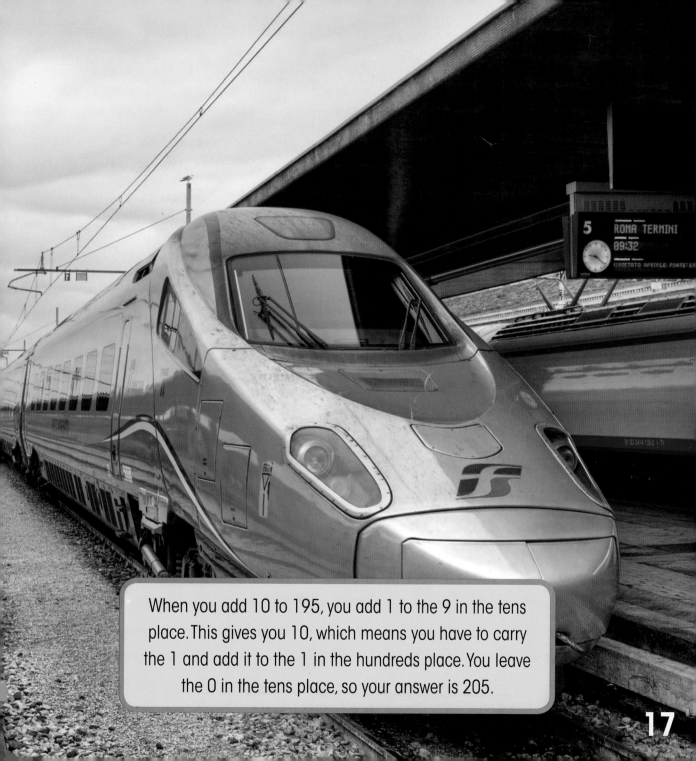

When you add 10 to 195, you add 1 to the 9 in the tens place. This gives you 10, which means you have to carry the 1 and add it to the 1 in the hundreds place. You leave the 0 in the tens place, so your answer is 205.

Railroad Records in China

The fastest passenger train, or train that carries people, is the CRH380A train from China. "CRH" stands for "China Railway High-speed." This train set the world record in December 2010 when it hit a top speed of 302 miles (486 km) per hour. When you subtract 10 from 302 in your head, you get 292.

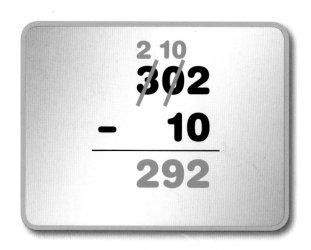

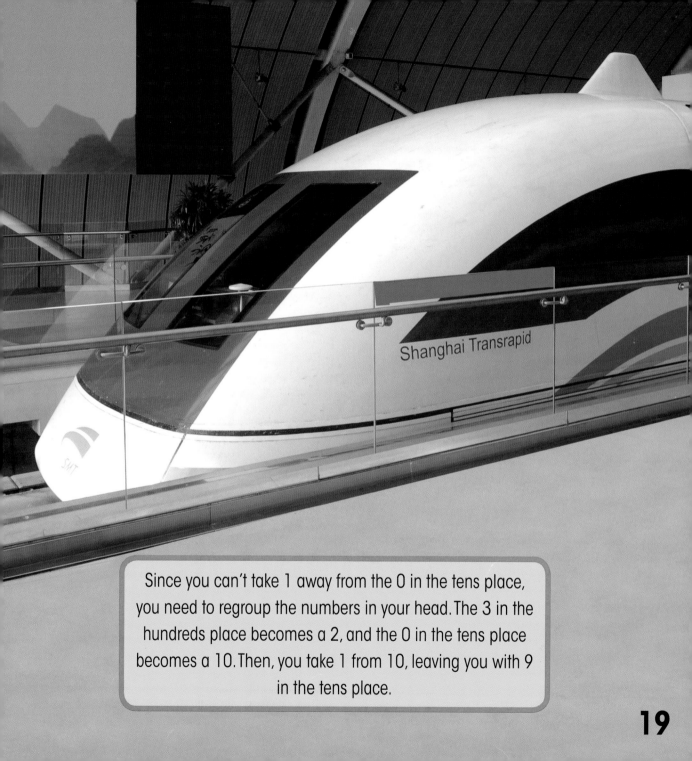

Since you can't take 1 away from the 0 in the tens place, you need to regroup the numbers in your head. The 3 in the hundreds place becomes a 2, and the 0 in the tens place becomes a 10. Then, you take 1 from 10, leaving you with 9 in the tens place.

China also has the longest system of high-speed train lines in the world. There are thousands of miles of rail throughout the country, and the Chinese government is planning for thousands more miles to be built in the future. Some high-speed rail lines in China are more than 900 miles (1,448 km) long. When you add 100 to 900 in your head, it equals 1,000.

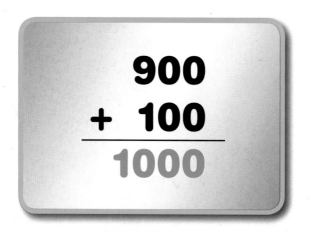

$$900$$
$$+ \ 100$$
$$\overline{1000}$$

Rail lines in China can be even longer than 1,000 miles. They **connect** parts of the large country that are far apart.

A Popular Way to Travel

High-speed trains are a helpful form of transportation. They keep the air cleaner than cars and airplanes. They also help keep roads and airports from becoming overcrowded.

There are no high-speed rail systems in North America yet. Until then, Americans can visit Europe and Asia to see what high-speed train travel is like.

In some places, high-speed trains can get people around so quickly that people choose to take them instead of airplanes.

Glossary

attract (uh-TRAKT) To make someone want
to do something.

average (AA-vuh-rihj) A middle point between extremes.

connect (kuh-NEHKT) To join together.

magnet (MAG-nuht) A piece of matter that is able to
attract iron.

popular (PAH-pyuh-luhr) Well liked.

transportation (trans-puhr-TAY-shun) A means or method
of moving goods or people from place to place.

Index

Due to the changing nature of Internet links, The Rosen Publishing Group, Inc., has developed an online list of websites related to the subject of this book. This site is updated regularly. Please use this link to access the list: www.powerkidslinks.com/mm/nobt/hstr